In The Color Of My Skin

Poems

Emmanuel Fru Doh

Langaa Research & Publishing CIG
Mankon, Bamenda

Publisher

Langaa RPCIG

Langaa Research & Publishing Common Initiative Group

P.O. Box 902 Mankon

Bamenda

North West Region

Cameroon

Langaagrp@gmail.com

www.langaa-rpcig.net

Distributed in and outside N. America by African Books Collective

orders@africanbookscollective.com

www.africanbookscollective.com

ISBN-10: 9956-764-75-2

ISBN-13: 978-9956-764-75-4

Dedicated to the oppressed in society, especially those victimized for their skin color.

To God Almighty Be Praise And Glory

Table of Contents

Preface

So much time has gone by since the days when only daring adventurers travelled the seas and returned with stories, sometimes fantastic, about their journeys and encounters, yet one thing that continues to baffle me today, is the portrait painted of Africa in the West. Africa is, in the West, especially the United States of America, the quintessence of disaster, virtually everything removed from human worthiness, the concretization of poverty and misery in a baffling wilderness. The continent's only acknowledged redeeming feature is her game sanctuaries—Kenya's Serengeti National Park, and South Africa's Kruger Park especially.

Given that people can easily travel to Africa and back if they really want to know the truth, although many are satisfied with these often ridiculous portraits painted by certain supposedly reputed newspapers and magazines, the media in general, I cannot help wondering what the charm is that keeps some Westerners enthralled by these remote, backward, and otherworldly portraits of Africa that they continue buying them. Yet this is the truth about how Africa is often presented in word or picture: that exotic, if not barbaric continent with bizarre ways, a place worthy only to be visited by the disturbingly inquisitive who, upon return after the very first visit, claim authoritative knowledge about the usually curious ways of the indigenes. The truth remains that the vast majority of open-minded visitors return to their native shores with fond memories of Africa, its uniqueness forever imprinted on their minds such that another visit is more likely a must. In spite of this, Africa's image remains, even in the twenty-first century, a charming, bewitching presentation of the remote, if not pristine past to many in the West.

Nevertheless, after close to two decades in the West, I have come to realize it is all about intentions, perspectives, goals, and benefits: what is one interested in depicting of another people, another culture, especially when endowed with the means to facilitate this construct.[1] Whatever the case, I am now convinced that the human being is happier in Africa than is the case in the West, all the propaganda and true material excesses of the latter notwithstanding. First of all, not all Africans are going around naked as the media houses of the West will want their citizens to believe, and their scanty clothing, indeed, becomes the weather conditions of the tropics just like the layers of thick clothing become the extremely frigid temperatures of the West. Secondly, Africans are not deficient of the meaning of real life, which is experienced in that warmth brought about by human beings living together, helping and loving each other, interacting with genuine concern for each other, without the manic fears and phobias of predators and stalkers that are routine in the West. I hope Africa can maintain this much longer with globalization and the effects it is having around the world as destructive cultures from wealthy nations are being branded as the zenith.

And so the propaganda of heaven on earth had us scuttling and rushing to the West to harvest of Eden, only to encounter another side of human nature largely alien to Africa—but for once upon a time South Africa—and worse even than Africa's trumpeted poverty and tribalism. In the West, I have experienced seething hate, and for no reason other than the color of my skin. For the first time, one encounters a culture where it is possible to be hated, dreaded, and avoided for no other reason than the fact that one is black. And the period spans the late 1990s into way past the beginning of the new millennium, 2016. Do not get me wrong, for I am going to do what the West hates to do when it writes about Africa by pointing out that there are exceptions to this claim: some of the men and women of the West are God's gift to humanity. This is obvious from their generosity and open-mindedness, which makes them willing to hear or learn the truth about Africa, a continent so frequently misrepresented if not deliberately maligned. Yes, Africa is a continent and not a country, and there is no language called African, at least as of now.

The result of the hate and mistrust is that in the West human beings are afraid of other human beings and so end up locked up in their homes, vehicles, or in themselves. I now understand better the claim that a dog is man's best friend, for what would become of most Westerners without their dogs, even as human beings abound as neighbors. Yes, it is in the West that human beings are so estranged from each other such that over something indeed stupid two neighbors quarrel so repeatedly, year in year out, until one of them just grabs a gun and shoots the other; so much poverty in the midst of plenty. It is worse today with technology overtaking human beings: one sees all categories of people locked up in their electronic gadgets instead of holding conversations. As a result, the family has collapsed, societies are collapsing, and God is now history, or at best largely irrelevant, as people twist the rules of life, the Ten Commandments, to suit their whims and caprices so that they can run wild with the desires of their bodies and ideological idiosyncrasies. They even dare to foist these eccentricities on other cultures around the world as they try to impose "freedom" and "democracy" on them, failing to realize the implications of cultural differences and the vast distinctiveness of human races and their environs.

At its most basic, it is said charity begins at home; nonetheless, here we are with so much to eat, yet afraid of others' shadows, let alone their voices: a place where one is immediately suspicious of another for being "too" friendly just because he or she greeted and asked after a stranger's day. And so I sing about this utopia with these wonderful doctrines and these daily experiences that tell me we are far from where we would like ourselves and others to think we are. I have come to learn that freedom is not free; it has shades if not layers, and even when won, it must be placed on the leash for its true worth to be enjoyed. I have come to learn that freedom must have a leash otherwise it runs wild and the human being degenerates to a point beyond animals even, leaving him or her spiritually and even physically unrecognizable. A child left to his own resources will burn his hand as he explores during his first encounter with a fire, gorge his eyes out with a knife he was playing with, or crash at the bottom of a cliff because he felt like or thought he could easily jump off. Freedom without regulatory rules is something else. Accordingly, as much as I would have liked to title these songs with a touch of freedom to it, I have chosen otherwise—a touch of color—because it seems to me to be that which defines our essence and experiences as black people wherever we happen to find ourselves beyond south of the Sahara. Hence the title, *In the Color of my Skin*.

LAMENT OF A BUSH-FALLER*

I am away from you
Not because I like it;
I am away from home
Because the music I danced
To was changing,
The rhythms unstable,
A hole in the palace drum.

I am away from home in search
Of steadier rhythms;
Those at home I tried to change,
With my life in danger from
Acolytes of the palace griot.

See then my departure
As clawing at straws for survival
Instead of a betrayal.

Remember, I have dipped
Into your waters and know the depths;
To my new shores a stranger you are,
Judge me not then in the distance.
My rhythms are new and
Strange, so anew I must begin.
Consider me not changed,
But a dancer with alien steps

---

* Bush-faller is a term used in Cameroon for all those who have left
the country to settle elsewhere in Europe or North America, especially the
latter though.

To which I must yield
Or else perish again.

From a distance my new
Rhythms are pleasant,
Pleasant to the ears and the eyes.
Come into the dance and see
For yourself: the steps are imposed;
Nothing spontaneous, a
Stranger to yourself you become
Again, clutching at straws
In the name of this dream.

More often than not it is
A Bush-faller's nightmare:*
The hours you must put in,
The Western Union calls
From the native shores,
And you dare not fail.

You my love must know
How hard for me the one to be
Doing all to stay connected
While all you do is nag
About days and moments of old,
With our bosoms in gentle embrace,
You think I have forgotten.

Show me the ocean without a bed,
The building without a foundation,
That nation without a history,
That soul without a past!

How then can I forget
Experiences that flowered me,
Moments that fashioned me?
No, for you I yearn every day,
For the once calm rhythms
Of our existence I long,
But how could I stay?
The old man needed a cane
A role I could not fulfill
With all the monstrosities in my path.

Outside this alien embrace,
For the python that must eat
Must crawl about sooner or later,
And the lion learn to roar
That someday must reign,
See me not as estranged
By choice, for the music, the music
Of *bush-fallism*....To listen to
It, is not to experience it,
To dance to it is to discover
The truth, so judge me not
From afar without tasting or listening.

DREAMLAND

The streets are beautiful
The houses sprawling warm
The people cold and damp,
Confused and hunting down shades;
Gripping fear and suspicion
Hold sway,
With loneliness King.

AFRICA SPEAKS

With my people it is known
A father does not lie to his son,
But here you tell my story
To your children
Not as it is.

You tell my story to suit
Your agenda, your whims and caprices,
Defaming me to your children,
Pointing the splinter in my eye
Forgetting the beam in yours.

I KNOW THAT RIVER

Look around, look around,
See for yourself to what times
Strange doctrines and beliefs have led.
In demand like some aphrodisiac harvested
In the cotton fields of history,
The whip skinning ebony hides the mea.
And transported for processing and extraction.

Today, look around and marvel.
In society one must dig hard
Into the belly of the hood
To extract just one.
With bloated sentences on their heads,
Being mere mules
Stupendous sentences on their lives,
Falsely identified for sowing and
Harvesting from blonde Edens: stowed
Away in the bellies of brick whales
Gray, or hastened on, even with
Heart rending pleas of innocence
Baked into another realm, or dosed off with
Countless mills of organ brake-fluid,
Not this hue, strangers to innocence
Plea rejected!

Hear the voices in the wind,
Of Nubian princesses wailing
In legalized solitaries, shacks,
Missing the warmth of their masculine bodies,
Like game hunted nearly into extinction.

Even then, see the pride of surviving manes
Strutting alienating streets, making ends meet
In a world mined against their efforts.

I know that river and have walked
The banks with my head held high.
I know that river, and have at times
Taken a dip, only a dip:
Unlike you, the rock planted in
Its bed with rising and falling tide.
The rock gathering all that moss
Of insults, as down on you they
Looked even without shame, the
Laws came and went, were bent
And straightened over and over
Maids at best to declare you
And nothing more, wolves that nurtured
Their young: cleaned them, napped them,
Fed them, only to be considered fit for the barn.

Yes, I know that river and can hear
Its songs through the reeds of labor
And hide on hide in the sun
Even after all the work in the fields
And the pain of a wife battered
A son and a daughter branded
Before the warrior castrated by
Chains of exploitative ingenuity.
I still hear the echoes, even today,
Of the Nile and the Mississippi battling
With lines, lines, yes lines.
I know that river.

IN THE COLOR OF MY SKIN

It is like a nightmare,
The practices of this civilization:
Many, so many look at me
And fake a smile,
Some choose not to see me, at all;
Like bats in daylight
They ignore me outright;
Talking to a dog instead.
I learned the problem
Is in the color of my skin,
Where I am from.
But can you hear the echoes of my
Laughter rumbling in the valleys of the scrapers?
Laugher at whitewashed ignorance,
Laugher at guilt masquerading as pride,
Laughter at culpability coated in complex;
Only the fool passes judgement
Down here below,
This insecurity in freedom,
Fearing the color of my skin
While missing out on the person.

FREEDOM

Real freedom has its periphery!
Yes, real freedom is not without restraint;
It is not like the mustang, its course,
Hills and valleys endless:
Here the blind claim to see
The deaf say they hear
Even the mute claim to speak,
All in the name of freedom.

The wind is truly free, yet its
Path has bulwarks and so
It bumps into trees and homes
With a strange fluidity
Belying the brashness of its encounter,
And the wind is truly free. So
Too Real freedom must have curves
To navigate, restrains, straps even.

True freedom must be guided
By the rules of decorum
Like politics by the constitution
And religion the commandments,
Instead of cascading ideological floods
Culminating in standards double,
Antagonizing and alienating even
If only to some: the sons and daughters
Of Melanin.

THE PORTRAIT OF FREEDOM

A pregnancy is usually welcome,
A happy event.
Though it brings with it inconveniences,
The parents look forward with excitement
To the arrival of their child,
And when at last it comes,
There is celebration.

Our child arrived after those marches,
But how can we be happy when
His growth is stunted,
His future made grim
With choked opportunities and
Traps snapping in his path?

Where then is his Technicolor coat
In the presence of conniving compatriots?
How then can we be happy
With the path to Pharaoh's kingdom,
The granary, blocked, even
With this raging famine?
How can we relish this victory
When ours is a mined path still,
Even with those fanciful terms
Of affirmed equity bandied around?
I hear the shouts of freedom,
The proud shouts of her beauty,
From other neighborhoods
Yet how my heart beats in fear each day
As my children leave home

To work, school, or play!
Some legal bullet might
Put an end to my life's work,
The love of my life,
Bring to an abrupt end my dreams,
Plunging a Marian blade into my heart thus
And argue for fear of his own life
He shot at a mere child with a toy gun,
He shot at a fleeing man in the back,
He choke-held to death a hustler,
Repeatedly tasered the handcuffed "hog"
To death right in front of the ER
Where he dared to run, handcuffed,
From the death-rider for help,
Or mistook a purse for a gun and shot to kill,
And did kill in fact,
And that blackanoid will
Be interred with little ado
Against a backdrop of
Administrative leave and brouhaha.

We claim freedom,
Why then is my heart this troubled,
Afraid of a system sworn my life to protect?

True freedom is deep and more than just words;
Beauty too runs deep … deep, deep down
Than what privileged tongues avow,
Deep, deep down
Than what meets the eye.

Freedom and God meet somewhere
Down the line, but where God has been
Banished, Where God is an alternative,
Oppression reigns, and with it
A weird form of freedom.
God must be present for freedom
To be freedom, real, and genuine.

CHANCES

When a people spend all their time
To make you look bad and
Out of place on God's earth,

When a people spend so much
Of their resources to make you
Look worthless here on God's earth

They assemble foul names and
Send them your way, call
Their crimes yours and jail
You for it, here on God's earth.

They'd rather you were dead
Than alive, and for no just reason,
Your image and character they
Assassinate, here on God's earth.

They retell and rewrite your history
To favor their ways while
Ridiculing yours for reasons
Unknown, here on God's earth.

They sleep with your women
They sleep with your men
And try to deny it but for
The *latte*, and smile with you
Only in private, here on God's earth.

Chances are, you are black.

THIS BURDEN

The sun will rise, the

Day and her events roll on
With that simplistic routine
At that deceptive pace,
With the impression that all is well,
All is as things ought to be.

Alas, behind certain names
Lie incredible forces at work,
Laying trees on innocent shoulders
The path of life making thorny,
Erstwhile simple and successful
Steps belabored with loaded sighs.

Forge on if you can,
Lending a hand here and there if you can;
Never another damn or ridicule.
These battles are mostly personal,
They are mostly personal
And so present otherwise.
That which meets the eyes
Is not always that which is.

A JOURNAL IN TIME

My heart bleeds
That you could genuinely hate
Without having known me before;
You just hate upon seeing me.

What did I do to provoke you?
I am the booty; you
Coerced others into the auction,
So how did I make you hate me?

Stowed away in the belly of your ship,
Chained and barely fed.
You cared not how sick I became,
Held incommunicado with look-alikes
Who spoke not my tongue.
My cross was heavy: loneliness,
Starvation, decease, and so I
Died and was tossed overboard.
So how did I make you hate me?

In every way humiliated, with chains
About my neck, you bid prices
Checked like domesticated game:
No bleeding gums, no dripping penis,
Healthy! Going, going, gone!
Sold, away from bonds
Built across that middle passage,
So how did I make you hate me?

In the cotton fields I labored, with
Lashes coursing the hide on my back
Even as the new black queen
Twitched in pain for me.
With her fierce black eyes
She told me how proud she was
Of me, as I hung from the stake
Bleeding quietly under the scorching heat.
So how did I make you hate me?

Within earshot, you raped my queen
And looked at me with scorn,
I could still see her proud black eyes
As with spite she walked past you to
Me. I got her message: You took
Her by force, against her will,
To me this beauty freely came.
How did I make you hate me?

Even when your frozen conscience thawed
And all the hoopla about freedom,
I was systematically pinned down
As I struggled to stand
With cowardly hoods,
Ashamed of your deeds, you
Intimidated me, and left me hanging
Stiff with blood trickling down my
Nose – strange fruit.
So how did I make you hate me?

Even after all this,
Falsely am I imprisoned, and
Without provocation, I am manhandled
And ultimately, frequently shot dead in the process,
Or else, with luck I rot in jail without evidence, but
One is as good as the other
And your public relations job is done.
You return home to your
Rouge wife and plump kids,
Mine alone, friend to her pain and tears,
My children embittered and frustrated
Dream of naught but joining me in jail
So how did I make you hate me?

Or is it the fear of your deeds?
Are you haunted by your heritage
And so would rather this front put?
Do not be an Iscariot, like Peter repent
And be pardoned.
My people know forgiveness.
We are one being's offspring
Whether you approve of it or not.
We have all in common, like it or not.
It may in size, length, weight, or color
Differ, but hair is hair
A head is a head
Teeth are teeth
A penis a penis
A vagina a vagina
So how did I make you hate me?

Your battle is with your conscience
And not with me.
I am long past that.
Be ashamed of your deeds
And repent when there is still time
Lest the Master's judgment be handed out.
I never made you angry.
You are your own worst enemy.

FAILING VALUES

How age has lost its weight!
Before, it was respect; it was power.
Those days ebbed away in time waves,
They can no longer be,
With pilfering seniors
In the name of politics,
With seniors now humpty-dumpties
In the face of evil,
Seniors squashing human lives
Like game. How can anyone
Still talk of values?
Integrity is dead, as Money
And Power reign in terror:
The new order,
The new standard.

THIS CIVILIZATION

Even after all the empires and kingdoms
Of old, I see today
Children having children
Raging gang wars sending bullets flying
And strays catching innocent victims
With daggers buried deep in flesh,
A pale ado and on
With drugs – traditional and modern
Zombifying morons and beasting others.
See the wars raging
On with modern philosophies
Of might is right
And mine is best….
What kind of civilization is this?

"THE FIRST WORLD"

In awe I look

At the shimmering lights
Of the city streets,
Street-valleys with towering hill-scrapers
The lighted mesh of rainbowed ribbons,
Sophisticated road networks,
Crowded by blinding headlights
Zooming past,

The overriding smell of fumes in the air
With partners' hounds off the leash.
Then that strange sterility by dawn
Of souls tormented by solitude:
In car-cells they zoom past
Afraid of their shadows,
Unable to smile, even at a neighbor,
For fear of legal claims
And stereotyped racial doubts.

Of what use are crowded skyscrapers,
Beautiful streets and condos tormented
By fear, suspicion, hate, and sickness?

What use these beautiful houses,
Their manicured lawns to fathers
Without any visitation rights,
To mothers overwhelmed
By total custody,
Offspring unbalanced and bitter

In between
In extremes emboldened by liquor,
Leaves, and even the needle?
And then a gun, a baseball bat, or
Simply off some bridge
On to the concrete waters below,
Splatter the pain.

The first world... mm!

APPEARANCES

Pardon me my love,
For the truth hurts yet must be told
That the tide may change for good.
We must all cry out and summon
To battle against our current vices
Towards a better generation
Than ours has proven itself.

How highly I thought of you,
Listening to and hearing the words of
Your founding fathers
With all the promises
The dreams of greatness and equality;
Alas, you are just another one
With a glittering difference.

After all I have heard and seen
From the children of freedom
From the land of the brave,
Between these shimmering shores,
You are just another savannah
With your Irokos housing rodents,
Your order and beauty stage props, roles
Chained to order by zooming squad cars.

I'd rather primitive
Than this developed,
A coward than this brave be.
This is some contagion,
With strange spices laced –

Sex, health, class, race –
Simmering on a strange hearth
Where family can barely bask
And compatriots chant joyfully
At the warmth of true freedom.

.

LAZARUS

The needy are everywhere,
In every land, clime, and culture,
So God alone knows why
They struggle to give the world
This is a Southern concept.

In every land on earth, there is a need
Even where people have surpluses.

They think because we go on foot
We are pitiable,
They think we have no canned food
So we are all starving,
They see us without woolen suits
And are convinced we are naked wretches.

But see these powerful yet nimble limbs,
With lungs of incredible capacities,
All from walking and running
Up and down the slopes.
They see me with pineapples from the farms,
Vegetables directly from the farms
And then they hear only of malaria
And cancer-less cells;
They learn it is because nature is my cook
And I am no wretch.
Africa is hot, my *boubou* is just right,
Blowing in the winds — the sails of the Sahara.
But today I hear strange rhythms invading my
Bedroom because of preservatives;

I hear strange echoes because of fertilizers,
And I can only watch as deformed
Death reigns imported
Even in aid packages, yet,
Not many can fly out to be chemotherapied.

See the march north,
Like colonial troops when first we met,
But these are soldiers battered by
The snowfall in the Sahara, with strange bodies
In their bodies—some never return,
Others casketed home.

When again shall I water drink from the leaves
And the *aŋkare*†burn in the fields?
When again shall I through the woods on foot
From one village to another, listening
To the drums in surrounding villages,
The rhythms echoing
About as I stride by—Paradise—with
The tables turned as they are today?

LIKE BLACK FOLKS DO

---

† Describes a system of farming where, during a new farming season, grass from farm beds is hoed into the furrow between old beds, covered with earth and then lit so it burns slowly with smoke rising into the sky.

I could never call this earth home,
Not only 'cos the bible calls me a pilgrim
But 'cos I have to moan and groan wherever I go,
Hoping I can educate and civilize
About my humanity.
Yet so much, just too much, is in my way:

The color of my skin the greatest bulwark,
I smile every day for God is no fool.
So you may try my life to turn into a nightmare
Yet I know the Master made all and He is no fool.
I am so equipped, above your triteness to rise,
That's why you see that trace of a smile
Framing my bold lips each time
I see you being a fool
By seeing only the healthy color of my skin,
Which you have maligned out of choice,
Instead of the person, the essence in me,
Just like black folks do anywhere on earth
Where this madness reigns.

AMIDST THE CIVILIZED

The only saving grace is the police,
Or so I thought and hoped.
In this world, age means nothing:
The young slight the aged,
They disrespect the cane
The races clash as they vie, one
Struggling to be on top of all else.

In this world the community has crashed;
Individualism is king and
Madness reigns on solitary minds
Stressed beyond limit by undisguised issues.

In this world secularism clashes
With spiritualism; the name "God"
Is taboo in public while Satan
Is celebrated everywhere by day and
By night, in public and in private,
Through orgies and more.

Ironically, with disaster people assemble,
They pray with lighted candles.
God is the spice for disasters, to be
Put away when normalcy returns.

In this world people treat all with
Suspicion, easily hating what they
Do not know, believing only
In themselves, sometimes disturbed even,
Life amidst the civilized.

RAIDS AND BRAIDS

(For you Justin)

You looked preoccupied in class,
And I wondered what the matter might
Be – I heckled you until you confessed
"I'm just hustling mein!"
"Don't mein me. I'm not your age, shit-head"
And Justin smiled knowingly. I was
Doing all because I cared;
I even called him "Son" and
He would smile with a
Glitter in his eyes, skin like oak,
Like a recognition he longed for,
With braids drooping past his neck.
"Stop hustling Justin, else it's gonna
Be jail or the grave someday soon."
He was beginning to listen to me,
To be focused.

Today, months after, I learned
He was in a summer vacation high-speed
Chase with the law. Nobody saw it come
To a close. Justin's body
Was later found in a dumpster.

Why would my blood pressure not rise?
Why would heartache not render
Me depressed and diabetic?
Why would all the damning statistics
Not be mine when you do the counting
And do the telling? Rest son of Jah,

He sees all and knows all and will reward us
For these untold manifestations
Of our whims and caprices.

BE LIKE FIRE ANTS

Step in the path of fire ants
And tell me what you experience,
Step in the path of fire ants
And tell me what they tell you.
Small as they may be, in their numbers
A force to reckon with:
They will make their presence felt,
They will bite you with mandibles so deep
You may have heads to chop off
To stop the pain.

Push a people too far and soon
They will fight back, my tale
To the circumcision age group:
Rush not to taste of bearded meat
Until the potency of thy plate is confirmed.
To be prepared is to guarantee certainty
To rush in with emotions only is to ascertain failure.
Patience is always a virtue even as the weak
Poke their fingers into your eyes
And insult you before your women.
A child does not rush out before it is term
Else its challenges begin even before birth,
So take your time and be sure
Which way is north and which south,
And then march on!

TAKING CHANCES AND TALKING FREEDOM

You just don't talk about serious things,
Like treating people like animals
Just because they look different,
In a way that makes no sense of your
Scholarly credentials Man!

You don't blame a people for their pain
When you've never known anything like it,
Your table overflowing with the fruits of their labor,
Spewing garbage about a people being lazy
Just because your spoon at birth
Was golden from slave paint,
And daily repainted by cheap black labor
As the years roll on to maturity.

You ridicule me at this hour?
While munching fruits from trees
Held in place by my sinews
And fertilized with my blood and flesh?

Test my hide and see what it can
And has accomplished under the cotton sun
And stake swing of your envious arm.
Today you dare call me lazy and self-pitying,
Even with the playing field still so tilted.
Let's into the field and see who
Will remain standing as the hours moan by.
How did you merit the loan
That was denied me?
You got the job even with

My towering credentials, and
I must always prove myself
Where you walk past as the norm,

And now you turn around without shame
To talk about my protestations as self-pity?
Pitting my lot against newcomers in the struggle
Now harvesting where I sowed singlehandedly
In bloody hours from dawn to dusk,
All now under the cloak of "minority,"
Harvesters whose path after yours I paved
With my sweat and blood.

A thief has no shame until caught;
Even then, the hardened become defiant
In their shame.
To call the sun the moon is to
Confirm your dishonesty.

FOR YOU MR. PRESIDENT (2015)

What charisma! The way you walk,
The way you talk, the way you smile,
I hear the screams in the distance.

It took more terms to bring down
This castle you inherited.
Where were the voices then that
I hear today in anger chanting jabber?
Now a new messiah in you
To rebuild in two penurious years
A castle that took eight and more to destroy
In the hour of surplus?

They see not the spangled banner
For once waved overseas
After a charred and trampling decade.
If only they would listen,
Listen to the rest of the world
A part of which they are
In spite of the ostriche they play,
They would see, they would hear,
And experience genuine admiration
Even at the dawn of your tenure
From shores that know.

It takes a mirror one's image to
See despite this jingoistic ruckus.

SO MUCH ADO ABOUT FREEDOM

How can I be free when
My essence is a trap waiting to snap,
My appearance an albatross hunted,
My existence made to haunt me down
With time and place for a crossbow

How can I be free when
My lifespan is hunting season
And I a stag in the background?
They say justice is blind
But then I go to jail for
Letting my dogs fight,
While you return celebrated with
The fights between men you organize
In posh settings watched on tubes
Around the world by celebrated numbers,
Or you with the uniformed gun
In your wake a black widow,
In your wake a black orphan.
And they let you walk,
Just doing your job
By turning our national shores
Into black killing fields.

You call this freedom?

THAT THING YOU DO

That thing you do,
Simply parting your lips
And baring your teeth
When you see me,
Is not to have smiled.

An honest smile begins from deep,
Deep down in the belly.
Like a burp
The ripples bubble up gently
To the surface,
Forcing the lips to part in honest appreciation
Of an Idea, a person: another human being.

That thing you do is a snarl
It threatens me instead.

BLOOD!

The blood of a chicken
Draws forth power from a lesser deity,
The blood of a goat or a bull
Draws forth power from a higher deity,
The blood of a human being is priceless
And causes the earth to tremble
And the heavens to rumble.

Yet, here I see human beings
Murdered on the whim,
A tranquilizer for a rampaging bear
A bullet for the setting sons of God Almighty
In the name of duty. And away,
Home to your milky spouse and
Downy kids, proud of yourself,
Even though there is a mother wailing
In pain for the untimely death of her son,
A young wife staring unseeingly at her
Now fatherless brood, dreading the
Symptoms of her once lively bed
All because of your cowardice
Your hatred for another race,
Another of God's creation!

This system may set you free, but
The judge whose sentence is without bias,
The judge whose sentence is without emotions,
The judge whose sentence is the truth,
Is yet to be confronted.
Not to believe in His existence

Is not to confirm His absence.
The deaf question the thunder's presence
Even as it rumbles on before the storm.
The blind cannot the lightning figure
Out, even as it streaks across
The horizon ushering in blizzards.

My people say at dusk by the hearth,
Passing on wisdom and our proud culture in tales:
Whatever you do unto others, you do to yourself,
Or else, someday, your children will reap the reward.

THE BLACK BURDEN

I do not eat seafood
But I eat fish.
I do not eat meat
But I enjoy barbecued ribs.
Drivers stop in traffic
For a bird and its family to waddle past,
Dogs are picked up from the streets
And abandoned homes and nursed
In to adoption with birds in guided flight
Back into the air, the wild,
The forest welcoming back its own
The ocean welcoming back her own.

Uniformed father, how is it
A kid playing with a toy is a threat to you
That you shoot to kill,
Or is it the color of his skin the threat?
An unarmed civilian shot in the back
And killed while trying to flee,
Another's head blown off
Behind the steering wheel
Just for being himself,
All by the supposed guardian of the peace
And in the name of fear
And nothing happens to them but
A paid break and subsequent recognition.
At best fired, jailed, soon to be paroled.
Human life from the South
Seems to mean nothing here.

CONVERSATION WITH A COP FRIEND

Of the Peelers, Jim,
Their land is free too, you know.
But they fail to rub it in like we do;
Instead of word of mouth, their actions
Show them keepers of the peace indeed.
Their actions confirm them civilized indeed.

With all due respect they will approach you,
With all due respect they will arrest you
After introducing themselves
And politely urge you come along with them
To the station.

Not so in this land of the free.
They categorize you first
And woe betide you if you are black,
The enemy, they declare war:
Swinging, dragging, choke-holding,
And slamming on the hard tarmac,
Icing the cake with a loud bang!

By your actions you declare yourself
An enemy, by your deeds you confirm
This declaration, yet demanding respect
And even sympathy and understanding
For your reckless butchering of civilians,
Of black civilians?

Civilians
Whom you swore to protect,
Killing of the innocent
With "dangerous neighborhoods"
Or fear for your life
Your liberation call.

Where are others who talk
And laugh like you?
Your colleagues come here
Barking out orders like dogs on heat
Bellowing out orders like castrated bulls
Shouting out at men and women indiscriminately
As if attempting humanoid domestication,
Spreading out hate like a hunter's bate
Spreading out discord like a farmer seeds,
Seeds of hate and discord in society
And then expect to be respected?

Hey Jim, courteous approaches
Will meet with courteous responses

But

When you come shouting
When you come swinging
When you come romancing your holster

Unprovoked,

Then I tense up
Ready to flee or fight;

Then I tense up ready to defend.

Rethink your approach
And I'm sure it will be different.
Respect is earned not demanded
You must show it to be given it.

Think human, not color,
And your work will be a lot easier
With civilians assisting, not hating,
As is the case with true
Peelers on their gentle island.

DEMOCRACY

If this is democracy
Then search and see if a
Better synonym for chaos there be.

To confront an elected president
With a loaded gun and call
This a display of rights.

To go on the air and disparage
A democratically elected president,
Victor of history's most tried elections
And call it a display of rights.

To flush the mind of every other
Word except "no" because to another
Party you belong; this is democracy?

To ridicule a president for erring
Like all else do, while brandishing
Him nude to a disgusted world
His tenure determined to blight and
Nothing else; this is democracy?

If this be democracy
Then ....

THIS CIVILIZATION OF CIRCUMSTANCES

Even after all the empires and kingdoms
Of old, ancient civilizations so to say,
Children having children
Raging gang wars with bullets flying
And strays catching innocent victims
With daggers buried deep in flesh
A pale ado, and on with drugs,
Traditional and modern,
Molding morons and turning others
Into monsters. See the wars raging on,
With modern philosophies of might is right;
This civilization!

And now with all those parents in jail
Some shot dead in the effort,
You legalize the crime
In the name of pain?

THE ECLIPSE
(*For Barack and Michelle Obama*)

Of forces, overwhelming forces,
And bodies superimposing victoriously
Of the elements
Making statements on nature and trends
Meteors of the era admired by the sane.
God Himself mankind is yet to satisfy
Not especially these stars,
Not especially these stripes of today.

From appreciative Puritanical forefathers,
From appreciative enslaved heralds
Determined but humble before the Trinity
To mere harvester of yesterday's fruits
Drunken by arrogance for founding labor;
When dry they pray and hunger for heavenly showers
To a God banished to the garbage heap
Of history and backwardness, primitivism,
Yet when at last it rains they complain.
Before it snows, for a white Christmas
They long and pray - pray…
When gently the dazed flakes begin
To descend they complain.

Then you? You? With those roots?
Son and daughter of the baobab?
Trunks of Iroko and the Ebonic sheen?
Spartacus Africanus! The stars may reject you,
With hypocritical attempts at frustrating,
But what has daylight in common with stars,

What has the sun in common with the moon?
Yet the rest of the world celebrated your warmth,
Yes, they ogled bewitched by your brilliance
And before Sheba trembled and cowered even;
Meteors of the age.

YOU AND ME

You swim home Olympian accolades
A role model indeed,
But your marijuana escapades
Are blamed on youthful ventures,
And jury pardoned.
For the same escapades Sheba's progeny
Is bullet riddled or caged,
Veritable upholders of the law.

You, at the helm,
You leave your wife and state
For foreign thighs and into a millionaire
Transformed with air time,
Sheba's son is dragged to court
And millions extracted for a milky gold-digger.

My siblings, mainly, pummel themselves
In a ring and this is big business
With hypocritical agents and promoters,
Yet because his dogs fought in a ring
That son of Jah tangoed with incarceration,
And post-corrections almost denied the right
To serve in the house,
Even with those unique moves.

You and I are so different before the law,
The standards so double
Even the blind can see and the numb feel it.

ILLUSIONS

Indeed it is a dream,
Even that which is concrete is not real.
I have a house, but it's not mine.
Break the 'gage and the truth will out
Until I have paid twice its value
To a faceless monster in my dream.

I have a car, but it's not mine.
Break the note and the truth will out
Until I have paid for at least two others
To a faceless monster in my dream.

Even my insurance policies are mirages;
I pay and pay from month to month,
But a percentage out of my pocket
Must co-pay my brief conversation
With the witchdoctor, remember?
In the end I have nothing,
It is mine as long as I respect the plan.

When my muscles shrink,
When my joints harden,
I am dumped where despair is partner;
Where all I do is tarry for transition.

My wisdom gained with the years
Waste away, I am now of no use
Even to my kids who barely
Remember to visit this liability.

THE SHAME OF FREEDOM

In freedom's airs we should all breathe freely
And nature's beauty and variety altogether enjoy.
To be free means to be equal before set standards,
No identity a source of sorrow should be;
No color a source of apprehension.

But here I am in shops closely monitored,
To the men and women of law and order
A classified criminal, even as the pedestrian
Walks over, across from me,
Else a fake smile on the lips.

Even though all aliens,
By generations separated,
I am always the outsider.
How else is freedom shamed?
How else is freedom ridiculed?

THE FARMER
(To the bushfaller)

I was taught to leave the house
And venture into the bushes
Meant a soul had a mission:
To begin a farm from the cleared lot.

He will hoe and nurture,
Chasing away birds, squirrels, and monkeys.
He will then harvest and bring
Back home the fruits of his labor.

Today is different: farmers forget to return home,
And like wretches, victims of strange spells,
Die in the fields, their bodies food for strays.
It were best they had not
Ventured forth from their navels.

SOCIAL CARNIVORES

How you relish heroes,
Fabricating them even from trivialities:
He saved a cat.

Then fan the flames of recognition
With your chorus echoing this feat and that,
So many grow fat around the story,
The hero himself now larger than life.

You pop his ego and deflate her image
With some hopeless story decades old;
It is the hour for dog to eat dog.
You slander, scandalize, and damn,

Reducing a once national hero into a mere rag
And then into the trash heap of history.
And on, this predatory culture marches
In search of the next victim.

To the wise, when those accolades begin flowing,
Remember the same tune will flush
You down the drain before long, and run.
Run!

WAITING TO BE SERVED

How my people have been played;
Ages have come and gone
Generations come and gone, yet
I see the same game unfold before me.

We are folks,
But people of a different kind,
To be treated with caution
Smiled at only when to be duped,
Looked at as a strange species
Belonging to a grade they designed.

Around the Sahara we treat them
Amicably, almost with reverence:
It is our culture to welcome the stranger
Even as his sand particles into our eyes
He casts.

Around the Antarctica they treat us
Like a plague, blight that tarnishes the snow.
And so they bare their teeth
In a failed smile that fools only them.

One would have thought "civilization,"
That word drummed and drummed
Would mean something else.
Would yield something better.

THE AFTERMATH

Long before my eyes my ears could see,
Our ways were like the rules of nature:
Firmly in place, nothing could move.
Then that fish puked
On our shores, and so began the
Journey into decadence.

Before you answered God's summons from
Beyond the clouds, *Teuhn* Njoya,
You thought you had seen it all,
Before your call *Nemoue* Kamah, you
Lamented the trends you saw, not
Knowing mere scouts they were.

I wonder what you would have done
Had God permitted you to see today?
Had He blessed you with a few more
Rains Kamah, I wonder what your
Lamentations would have sounded like,
As you question today's offspring's origins.

Now Angwi sits in the midst of men,
Elders, hanging her legs miles apart, like a man;
Nfor walked past me yesterday,
Looking at me straight in the eyes
But will not greet;
This morning Fonyuy spat back words
Into his father's Mouth – they are now age mates.

Today's red feathers no more value seem
To possess with elders now telling lies,
Stealing from the palace even.
I have seen calabashed palm-wine rejected for
Liquid in a bottle, and watched
Ngwe eat *achu*[†] with a spoon as men
Look on with nothing to eat.

Whose ways are these?

[†] Achu is the traditional dish of the Ngemba peoples of the Bamenda
Grassfields of Cameroon. It is eaten with the index finger mainly.

THOUGHTS OF THE WOURI BY THE MISSISSIPI

By the river whiling time,
By the river ruminating on life
With the smell of burning coal
In the air from nearby barbecuing:
Fish, chicken, or beef, I could
Not tell nor see to tell.

But from my towel-mat by the river
I thought of their reaction should I dare:
"Can I join in the barbecuing?" I wondered
If a hooded glance would be the answer
After all the social battles
I am now familiar with.

Back home by the Wouri, I know we would
For sure: "Oh, sure join us."

We have our faults and they are many
But we are different,
We are a people that feels
We are a people that understands
We are a people that knows how to love
We are a people that's got soul.

THE MISSING LINK

There is everything here, virtually,
Everything one could ever possible need,
Yet how so empty and needy I feel.

There is food of all kinds,
From north to south,
From east to west of the globe,
Yet we hunger for vitamins.

So many and diverse are the humans here
But always trapped behind walls,
Walls of glass, metal, blocks, sheetrock,
Walls of fame and fear, fright even.

When we venture out,
We walk past humans without even a word.

In these excesses, there is so much want,
The bodies and the souls of so many
Ever so restless.
In these excesses God is missing,
At best locked up in churches
Released only to be blamed when
A soul snaps and bullets score homeruns
Or some other calamity makes a touchdown.
Of what use is a person without the soul,
What use a society without God?

And so with so much we are so sad:
His commandments we have fossilized

His name into a curse turned,
The Sabbath loaded with labor,
In vain watch for dawn.

The soul must again bow before that name
For life and death to have meaning,
Else in vain we labor.

THE AFRICAN FAMILY IN THE DIASPORA

From a land rich in values
We touched the shores of freedom
Drenched in hopes of success,
Immediate wealth.

Before long we drink drunk
Of ideas, and slowly, slowly
Values corroded that which for generations
Have held many in awe:
Wives begin snarling,
Feeling comfortable with kitchen-husbands;
Our children begin talking back
Brandishing the phone in one hand,
Freedom's passage ushering in
Impatient cuffs and guns.

Slowly I recognized not myself any longer
In this land of the free
With the members of my family
In entropic co-existence as once
Established roles and structures are starved
As hierarchy shrivels and dies,
Choked by freedom.

In the diaspora,
Our wives send their husbands packing
With children retorting to their parents.
The lion roars without the echo in return
And laments this alien turf
Where cubs piss and shit

On the mane without consequences.

The dishes pile up in the sink
As they gallivant in and out,
The car through yesterday's dirt peeks,
The wife remembers not
The smells of her kitchen
And no longer cares about
The looks on an eating husband's visage,
With restaurant knobs in her grip.
The father eats there and then
She herself eats here and there;
The children, who knows where and when?
Apart, unbridled freedom pulls and pulls
And at last it snaps. With State backing
She shouts back,
Dishing orders at her State emasculated bullock
Until he can take it no more;
The rings clatter on the floor.

Too late when she sees the value of
That original biblical structure
Ingrained in our roots, of the father
As the head and the mother the neck.
By now anxious young manes
Have lapped and lapped,
The pleasure fades into nonsense
With the spraying of their identity,
Juices of victory over the alienated throne
Of once upon a black mane, without the
Public will to claim ownership.
The ageing lioness, now with numerous

Anxious brown manes at her disposal
Yet she is bitter, something is missing,
Even as the kids distance themselves from her
Ashamed of her newfound companion—freedom!

A HUSBAND'S LAMENT IN THE DIASPORA

Back then, when I spoke, those about me,
The children, especially, hushed.

Back then, when I spoke, everyone listened;
They did not look at me in the face.

Back then, when I spoke,
They all stood before me
In humble submission, respecting
The number of broken utensils I have,
Knowing that I am their father,
Acknowledging that I am the husband.
How close we were, how strong the family;
Now, I see wonders in this house:

My children look me in the eye
As if we are of the same age-group,
They try to talk back when I talk to them,
They say they have their own opinions too.
Even their mother says she is tired
And wants me to go into the kitchen.
And then they pick the telephone
And call strangers into my house
To talk to me about bringing up my children
As if I did not learn anything from my parents,
To talk to me about my wife's rights
As if I did not experience my parents love for each other.

61

With my hands now tied,
The laws of freedom and equality,
The kids go and come, ignoring
What they call a curfew,
The young laughing when I *ground* them,
Their thing,
Instead of the cane or picking the pin.
What can I do my people,
What can I do
Since I cannot whip them
Like my father did to save me from
The monster I was already becoming?
I go without food since the wife is tired
And wants me to take turns in the kitchen,
What can I do since I cannot raise my voice at her
Without a sentence for domestic violence?

If I had whipped you yesterday you would
Not have been handcuffed and shot at today;
If you had remembered that you felt pride
In cooking for your family no matter what
Before you heard of 9-1-1, where would
The thought of another wife have come from?

And so we have gone our separate ways,
Now the children can eat and do whatever
With their opinions; you, my wife, their mother,
Can now rest for as long as you want
And let the government pay the bills I paid,
Let the government buy the cars I bought
For you when you cooked for the family. Today
I have found me a woman who remembers

Her roots. She cooks for me her husband
No matter what, and I do for her all that
I used to do for you and our children.
I do think of you all, from time to time,
But I am now about as happy as I was with
You all but without the fear of the phone,
Without the threat of 9-1-1 calls and squad cars
At my door. We are thinking of children,
But we will wait until back home, where
We can bring them up the way we were,
With tough love if need be, than wait
For the police to lock or kill them. We
Both know where we came from.

Now with angry children in between
Because you chose to follow the Romans
While ignoring your tradition which
With roles held the family together,
At last you are free and no longer tired, I hope.

I hear now you have a different man every night
But you are yet to find me in them,
And so I hear you cry day after day for what used
To be before freedom and equality invaded our family.
How is it then that with your fleece
In your hand you still shed tears?
Freedom!

WORDS TO A BLACK BOY

On your toes must you stand,
Walking on eggshells, with gazes
Like arrows piercing your stir.
Do not ask me why Son, for
I wonder myself from time to time.

You must this cross bear
Like the Master's His Father's will
In spite of the Sanhedrin.
You must this cross bear
With dignity, refusing to fall
Into the trap-pools surrounding you.
You must stay calm and
Walk with your head in the clouds
'Cause that's where you belong
In your pride – Mother Africa!
Define yourself else another's
Phobias will. Our lives Son are
Different, let nobody tell you otherwise.
I know the Lord knows and is
Watching though—so be still!

ON JUDGING LIVES

From a distance, a comfort niche,
Life looks like a plain field.
Inch in closer and you will better
The hills and valleys notice.

From afar, a comfort zone,
Life looks like a large body of water.
Come in closer and the huge waves
Threatening the heavens notice.

Even with the rain clouds gathering,
From far off you will think all is gentle;
Move in closer and the ugly head of
A storm will reveal otherwise.

Level not then the terms of perception,
The parameters perceiving achievements.
Instead commend all for staying alive
For being able to interact.

Our real lives, struggles, goals, and achievements
May never meet the human eye.

EVOLUTION

For long,
Messing with our brains,
I have been called names
For being who—what—I am,
A fact I never had a problem with.

Boy: The commandant and the
Captain with their cheating
Wives, sharing sex like candies to the
Neighborhood men from yonder.
Lazy as they are,
Can't lift a finger to wash her own
Drawers even: I washed, cleaned
Cooked – boy! Their debauched
Orgiastic lives in my hands; I smiled.

Kaffir: Even on my own turf, as they
Steal from my mother's breast and
Rape and plunder all about with
Bullets for us, the world looked away
In hypocritical silence, else chanting the
Holocaust of yore instead; I smiled.

Negro: My notorious feature is my nose
Not pointed like an eagle's beak
And so they harped on it forever.
I have never had problems breathing;
A broken nose is hardly my call; I smiled.

Black: Is the problem with my eyes
Or with a people who refuse to know
The value of peculiarities?
I thought we are all shades of
Chocolate, even extremely dark, but
Black is preferred; I smiled.

Monkey: I have taken all without protest.
This I refuse to take: some monkeys and
Gorillas are black with nostrils not pointed.
Face it, whose hair is like a monkey's?
Whose pony tail a horse's mane?
Whose hair is like that of a canine?
Whose body covered with long unsightly
Hair it must be shaved? Not kinky!

Show me the truly human then!

AFRICA LOOKS BACK

Yesterday they arrived unannounced
And protested because of my wives,
With tales that only one is the right number.
Today these same people tell me
Another man could take her place.
See a people who know not the difference
Between a man and a woman,
Between a husband and a wife
Telling me how to run my home.

SETTING SAIL

Once upon a time a humble people,
With the fear of the Lord their core,
In Him they trusted and counted
And so from Puritanical nothing
Soared to the foremost.

Alas, today's overflowing barns
Engender arrogance even
Towards Him who fashioned their success,
Towards Him who gave all that the
Founding Fathers prayed for with reverence.

And so now their progeny
Harvesting in opulence from
Whence they did not sow,
Knowing not the price of hard work,
Knowing not what it takes to
Be true children of the Father, have
Banished Him from their midst, with
Scientific creators boasting causes and effects,
Unable gratitude or plea to accord the Master.

In their paths then icebergs strewn
And now the titanic is tipping
And a time, at this pace, will come
When the ocean's floor shall plays host
To splattered wealth, and waves
Regurgitate jetsam and flotsam,
Prints of once upon an Ozymandias.

CHILDREN OF DIOSPYROS

Offspring of Diospyros,
With limbs like the Baobab
Trunks like the Iroko
With statures like the Obeche
Harvested from my Mother's breast
Before prime and exploited at large.

We've waded inhumane tides
And emerged stronger, but
We must now begin to look back
Even to our blighted roots
With these microbes still milling
Deeper and deeper into our essence.
Lose the hurt and the anger
Set goals and patiently pursue.

Break that grip Africa
And put your sons and daughters
Princes and princesses where they belong -
Pedestals!
Mother, break that grip
From the hands of pilfering aliens
Pretending cooperation.
This had been our tragedy, from slavery,
Then colonialism, neocolonialism
And now globalization aka alienation
From our proud roots infested by maggots,
Our albatross the color of our skin.
But with these lines
To you as an individual

Begins the end of our woes
As we refuse to fall any lower.

These seeds of hate
These seeds of inadequacy
Are layers of ideologies
Drummed, whipped, injected
Into our minds and bodies
And non other than we ourselves
And our trust in God Almighty
Can free ourselves from these shackles.
Ours has been the story
Of the very best seeds
Winnowed beyond by brutal forces
Of exploitation and abuse, but the hour is now.

RIDDLES

In this realm, at this hour
When Ebony limps in a backwater
Predicament, laws are for the poor
Rules for the oppressed
Shades of lawns for the wealthy
Meaningless riddles for the favored
To laugh and mock at the outcome
Of chases, murders, and suits
In a game called Justice
In a game called Freedom.
All striped by shades.

MANDELA'S MESSAGE

Let time flow by like the Niger
Let the hurt sink in like microbes
Patience must be the key
And not a mere desire your hurt to prove
In a reckless fit of rage.

You must be patient, take time
Your opponent to study
And his ways master
Educate yourself, conscientize your likes
And then engage.

It may take time but vice could
Never the victor forever be,
Its victory is ephemeral
In the end it must bow out
In a battle against virtue.

Printed in the United States
By Bookmasters